D0516471

My
FUTURE
CAREER

Working in the

Fashion Industry

Margaret McAlpine

GARETH**STEVENS**

GS

P U B L I S H I N G
A WRC Media Company

Please visit our web site at: **www.garethstevens.com**
For a free color catalog describing Gareth Stevens Publishing's
list of high-quality books and multimedia programs, call
1-800-542-2595 (USA) or 1-800-387-3178 (Canada).
Gareth Stevens Publishing's fax: (414) 332-3567.

Library of Congress Cataloging-in-Publication Data

McAlpine, Margaret.
    Working in the fashion industry / Margaret McAlpine.
        p. cm. — (My future career)
    Includes bibliographical references and index.
    ISBN 0-8368-4774-1 (lib. bdg.)
    1. Fashion—Vocational guidance—Juvenile literature.
    2. Clothing trade—Vocational guidance—Juvenile literature.
    I. Title. II. Series.
    TT507.M27   2005
    746.9'2'023—dc22   2005042524

This edition first published in 2006 by
Gareth Stevens Publishing
A WRC Media Company
330 West Olive Street, Suite 100
Milwaukee, Wisconsin 53212 USA

This U.S. edition copyright © 2006 by Gareth Stevens, Inc. Original
edition copyright © 2005 by Hodder Wayland. First published in 2005
by Hodder Wayland, an imprint of Hodder Children's Books.

Editor: Valerie Weber
Inside design: Peta Morey
Cover design: Melissa Valuch

Picture Credits
Corbis: Roger Ball 17; Peter Barrett 40; B.D.V. 39; Petre Buzoianu 21; Steve
Chenn 15; Condé Nast Archive 45; Valerio De Berardinis 53; Stephanie Diani 23;
Firefly Productions 56; Kevin Fleming 10; Owen Franken 5; Steven E. Frischling 52;
Mitchell Gerber 20, 22, 43 (bottom); Rick Gomez 19 (top); Dave G. Houser 13; Jose
Luis Pelez, Inc. 16; Michael Keller 31; Jutta Klee 29; LWA-Stephen Welstead 6; James
Leynse 57; Gail Mooney 14, 37, 54; Mark Peterson 59 (top); David Raymer 48;
Chuck Savage 12; Zack Seckler 47; Ariel Skelley 19 (bottom), 36, 59 (bottom); Paul
A. Souders 7; Henri Tullio 30; Patrick Ward 43 (top); Michael S. Yamashita 9. **Corbis
Sygma:** Jeremy Bembaron 51 (left); Vo Trung Dung 8; Yves Forestier 38, 41; Pace
Gregory 25; Eric Robert 46; Siemoneit Ronald 51 (right); Cardinale Stephane 32.
Getty Images: cover, Evan Agostini 33; Steve Finn 35; Sean Gallup 4; Peter Kramer
49; Klaus Lahnstein/Stone 55; Arnaldo Magnani 11; Zoran Milich 34; Patrick Riviere
28; Toru Yamanaka/AFP 24. **The Image Works:** Frank Pedrick 27. The Image
Works/Topham 44. TopFoto/UPPA 26. **Note:** Photographs illustrating "A day in
the life of . . ." pages are posed by models.

Printed in China

1 2 3 4 5 6 7 8 9 09 08 07 06 05

Contents

Words that appear in the text in **bold**
type are defined in the glossary.

Display Designer

What is a display designer?

Display designers create exciting, inviting product arrangements to attract customers. Display design starts at the front of a store, often in large windows. After customers are lured inside the store, smaller displays help persuade them to stay and buy the products used in the displays. Display designers also create displays for large **trade exhibitions** that showcase the products of specific industries.

Depending on the departments or stores they work in, display designers pull together different objects to create a complete look. Designers for a home-furnishing store, for example, may feature a dining room display, with a table, chairs, plates, and silverware. In a clothing store, a dress on a hanger may not attract much attention, but when the same dress is on a **mannequin**, with **accessories**, it catches customers' eyes. The display gives them an idea of how the dress might look on them.

Stores do not want to bore customers, so displays are changed frequently. Often, displays reflect different

Attractive window displays bring customers into stores. Many clothing stores have an individual look that customers will recognize immediately.

Plate-Glass Windows

In 1834, British manufacturer Robert Lucas Chance used a process developed in Germany to produce large panes of glass. This process was used widely to make plate-glass windows. Stores use these large windows to show their products in displays that will attract the attention of people passing by.

seasons or holidays. In December, for example, displays may show festive foods, gifts, and clothing for Christmas, Hanukkah, or Kwanzaa.

National chains of stores need to have each of their stores look fairly alike. This similarity helps make sure that customers recognize a chain's stores across the country. It also promotes customers' loyalty to store brands. Head designers for national chains work at the company's corporate office. Their instructions and their chosen materials are sent out to individual stores where the local display designers set up displays, according to the head designers' instructions.

The huge Mall of America, in the state of Minnesota, contains hundreds of stores. Many of these stores sell similar goods and compete for the same customers. Without good display designers, stores may lose customers to their competitors.

Main responsibilities of a display designer

Display designers are responsible for customers' first impressions of stores. It takes a lot of work to create an atmosphere that customers will appreciate and enjoy. The designer might want a relaxed, country-style atmosphere, for example, and use pale wood and soft colors to achieve that. At the other extreme, the designer could try for a bold look, using black-and-white materials and shiny **chrome** fittings. Whatever the style of a store, the displays need to reflect it.

Choosing the colors and fabrics for a display is not easy. The designer must have a clear idea of the mood he or she wants to convey and pick the materials and colors that will express that mood.

At the planning stage, designers work closely with store managers and **buyers** to decide on:

* displays that will most appeal to customers
* the **budget** for each display
* dates during which a display will stand

The designer then:

* sketches some initial designs by hand or creates them using a **design program** on a computer

Good Points and Bad Points

"My job is very creative, which is great, but pleasing everyone can be difficult. Sales managers often have products they want to promote, and pulling these different items together in a pretty display isn't easy."

- shows the initial designs to the store managers and department heads for approval
- finds the materials needed to make the final display

Designers often put together much of the display themselves. Some displays may be quite simple — for example, using elements such as drapes in the background with huge photographs in front. Others create an elaborate scene or series of scenes linked together and telling a story. Many stores now use what is known as retail theater, which creates a total environment appealing to many of the senses. Once a display is in place, design staff are responsible for cleaning and repairing it and for taking it down for the next display.

This window display designer is dressing a mannequin in a **boutique** in Vancouver, Canada.

Main qualifications of a display designer

Artistic skills
Display designers need to be creative and artistic, with a good eye for color and whether a display is pleasing to the senses.

Imagination
Designers need to be able to come up with plenty of new ideas for eye-catching displays.

Computer skills
Designers need to be confident computer users because they often have to use design programs on a computer.

Designers often sketch out a number of their ideas for more complex displays. Then they can choose from their options.

Technical skills
Although stores employ carpenters and electricians to help install large displays, most designers are expected to work on the displays themselves. Only the most senior designers working for large stores or retail chains have other designers to put displays together.

Their work includes:

- using tools to construct displays
- understanding how lighting systems work
- dressing mannequins, setting up furniture, and arranging flowers and other **props**

Stamina
Designers are on their feet for much of the day, bending, lifting, and stretching. They need lots of energy because the work can be physically tiring.

Teamwork

Designers must be able to work as part of a team of people. For example, they need to discuss with buyers and managers what effect they want to achieve from a display before they start to design it. They also work closely with other people throughout the project.

Communication skills

Designers need to talk over their designs and listen closely to other people's ideas.

Tact

Designers may have to explain why other people's ideas would not work in a display. They must be able to do this tactfully and without causing offense.

fact file

There are no formal requirements for display designer positions, although some designers may have bachelor's degrees. Their background is often in art or design. In a job interview, they will be required to demonstrate how well they can communicate their ideas and a keen sense of design, line, and form.

A display designer adjusts a scarf. Shoes, scarves, ties, and other accessories show customers how they may want to complete an outfit.

Robert Morden

Robert is a junior display designer at a large department store. He is one of three young designers working under a senior display designer. He got his present job soon after graduating from college.

8:30 a.m. I'm at work early today, so I walk around the outside of the store checking the window displays. A few of the mannequins need some adjustments.

9:30 a.m. The emergency repairs are done, and I'm in a meeting where the design and financial teams are talking over the display budget.

11:00 a.m. I receive a phone call from the evening-wear department. A customer wants to purchase a dress from the display. Clothes are not usually sold from the displays because it is a lot of work to remake the display. This customer's dressmaker did not finish a dress for her on time, and now, she doesn't have time to order a new dress. Our store tries to find the dress on display in her size. Our manager even phones another one of our stores nearby to see if it has one. Meanwhile, I talk to my boss about a replacement for the display.

Displays may reflect the season or a holiday — in this case, Christmas.

In 2000, this New York City department store used real people as models in its Christmas window display. Each of the store windows focused on a decade from the twentieth century.

12:00 p.m. **Customer service** wins the day, and the dress is sold. I start to take the display apart, removing all the pins and foam pads without causing any damage to the dress.

1:30 p.m. I have a quick lunch and think over my new display. It doesn't involve a complete window, but the accessories will need to be changed.

2:15 p.m. The manager shows me three dresses. I make a final decision and choose new accessories and props from different departments in the store.

4:45 p.m. My boss sees the display and says I have done a good job, so the day has a happy ending.

5:15 p.m. I clean up, putting my pins, foam pads, and other display materials back into my workbox.

Fashion Designer

Fashion designers develop new ideas for clothes, which are then sewn into actual garments and produced for sale. Some fashion designers create their own lines of clothing, and others work for manufacturers who produce clothing for a large **market**.

A designer checks a piece of fabric against a design on his computer. He wants to see if the fabric would look good with his latest design.

The world of fashion depends on **trends**, which change frequently. Specific colors may be fashionable for several years and then go out of style. Patterns of material change as well; one year, **paisley** or another distinctive print is in fashion, and the next year, bold, geometric patterns are everywhere. Designers must make sure their design collections reflect popular trends, so they research and plan carefully before starting design work. It can take two years from the time a designer develops an idea to the time the finished garment appears in stores.

Fashion designers visit **trade fairs** and fashion shows to find out which styles, fabrics, and colors are likely to be popular. With this background, they can combine their design ideas with current trends.

From High Fashion to High Sales

Isaac Mizrahi's fashion designs are fun, clever, and colorful. He began his career designing expensive clothing sold only to the wealthy; Madonna and Oprah Winfrey wore several of his outfits. He later moved into designing for mass production. Mizrahi now designs everything from bedding to women's sportswear to dog collars, all of it at affordable prices.

Fashion design falls into different areas, including:

- **haute couture**, where designers display their work to customers, who then buy garments made specifically for them; one outfit may cost thousands of dollars
- **ready-to-wear** collections, where designs are produced in small numbers and sold at high prices in select stores
- **mass production**, where designs are manufactured in large numbers and sold at reasonable prices in stores nationwide; most designers work in this area
- **boutique** design, where designers work alone or in small teams, creating their own designs and finding outlets to sell them

Many designers hope to work for one of the world's great **fashion houses** such as Chanel. Fashion houses sell their own designs.

Main responsibilities of a fashion designer

Designers often specialize in a particular branch of fashion. They may design outerwear, such as coats and jackets, or lighter clothing, such as dresses, suits, and **separates**. They may create wedding dresses, or they may specialize in menswear.

The first step for designers in any field is to determine their clients' needs or what would appeal to a large number of buyers. Their second step is to sketch their early designs, either on paper or using a computer. They consider different fabrics and colors and whether various design elements will work together. How will a wool fabric look trimmed with leather? Will this shade of yellow look good next to the green that is fashionable this year?

Some designers specialize in creating exciting, unusual, and beautiful shoes.

Good Points and Bad Points

"The fashion industry is so exciting, and I get a real buzz out of being part of it."

"Many people want to work in fashion because it looks so glamorous. The number of talented people applying for this work makes the field very competitive. I'm only as good as my last design. What if it doesn't sell? I could be out of a job."

Designers who run their own small businesses, like the ones shown above, cut and sew the fabric for their own designs themselves. Designers employed by large fashion houses have teams of garment workers to do that work.

The third step is to produce the most promising of these designs and try them on models. In large organizations, garment workers sew the designs, but in small companies, the designers do it themselves. At this stage, designers usually make many changes to the form and style of the garment. Clothes look very different on a real, **three-dimensional** person than they do as a design sketched on a page. In the mass-production fashion industry, garment workers sew sample clothing, which is shown to possible buyers. The most popular styles then go into production. The designer advises on any changes required by the mass-production process.

Main qualifications of a fashion designer

Artistic skills

Designers need to be both creative and original to keep one step ahead of other designers and produce fresh lively designs that reflect the mood of the moment. Sometimes a film, event, or geographical area, such as Africa or India, captures the public imagination, and fashion designs reflect it. Designers must consider current interests and use their eye for color, line, and form to turn these interests into popular fashion designs.

Technical skills

Designers need technical skills to make their ideas reality. These skills involve:

- the ability to make clothing patterns out of designs
- a good knowledge of different fabrics and how they can be used
- the ability to sew to understand the different techniques that can be used to create clothing

Designers sometimes find it useful to discuss their ideas with their coworkers. Many designers keep their designs secret, however, so others do not use these ideas themselves.

Computer skills

Designers must be confident computer users with an understanding of **design programs** so they can make changes to their designs quickly. With a computer, a designer can see almost immediately how different colors look when used together or how changing short sleeves to long sleeves with cuffs could change the appearance of a dress.

Business skills
Self-employed designers must know how to manage a business, making sure they do not spend more than they earn and contacting possible clients.

Self-confidence
The fashion industry is tough and competitive. Designers need to believe in their own abilities so they can cope with criticism and disappointment.

Discipline
Designers must work independently, meet dead-lines, and keep to **budgets**.

Communication skills
Designers must be able to explain and describe their work to other people.

fact file

Most employers in the fashion world look for people with two- or four-year degrees in art and design or fashion. They must also know about various fabrics, **accessories**, and trends in the world of fashion. Beginning designers can expect to spend several years working on other people's designs before designing clothes themselves.

Students of fashion design must learn how to measure, cut, and sew patterns. They learn how clothes are made before creating designs themselves.

A day in the life of a fashion designer

Susie Harris

Susie runs her own business designing and making wedding and evening gowns. After graduating from college, she worked for a company specializing in evening wear. She felt she had learned enough about the design and business side of the work to set up her own company after five years.

7:30 a.m.   I'm altering a dress because the bride has suddenly lost a lot of weight, and the dress no longer fits just right.

9:00 a.m.   I visit one of my **freelance** garment workers to talk about new assignments. I do a lot of my own detailed sewing, such as embroidery, but I also need skilled people to sew for me. So far, I have a team of three who work out of their homes.

11:00 a.m.   I have an appointment with a new client and her mother. They have cut out pictures from magazines, drawn sketches, and collected fabric samples, so they are quite clear about what they want. The fabric they have in mind is too heavy for the style, which has a full skirt and a tightly fitted waist. I explain that there could be a problem and suggest I find new fabric samples.

1:00 p.m.   No time for lunch, so I eat a quick snack in the car.

2:00 p.m.   I meet with a writer who wants to interview me for a magazine article. One of my dresses was worn to a big wedding. The event was described in the newspaper, where the magazine writer read about me. A photographer from the magazine is coming to see me next week, which is great!

4:30 p.m.   I'm back at the cutting table. I need to finish cutting out the pattern for this evening dress today so I can deliver the pieces to my sewing team at their homes.

6:00 p.m.   I receive a phone call from someone who wants me to design a ball gown. It has been a good day.

Clients may have firm ideas of what fabrics and styles they want before they meet the designer.

Designers are often self-employed and handle all the various areas of their businesses, including taking orders and sewing their own designs.

Fashion Makeup Artist and Hairstylist

What is a fashion makeup artist and hairstylist?

Fashion makeup artists and hairstylists apply models' makeup and style their hair for fashion shows and **photo shoots**. Fashion makeup artists and hairstylists are also known as fashion stylists.

A glance at any photograph in a fashion magazine shows the importance of makeup and hairstyling in the fashion world. In everyday life, makeup and hairstyles are usually simple and practical. Fashion styles are much more elaborate, created to **enhance** the garments being displayed. Sometimes the hairstyles and makeup worn in fashion shows and photographs are extremely dramatic. Stunning, unreal designs create an air of complete fantasy.

A fashion model waits backstage at a show for her makeup artist to arrive.

One of the biggest differences between working in a beauty salon and in the fashion industry is the speed at which fashion stylists work. In a salon, hair stylists can take time to make sure customers are satisfied

A makeup artist works on a model for a fashion show in 2004. It takes a lot of planning to create an unusual and eye-catching face with makeup.

with the results of their work. During a fashion show, models change outfits quickly. Fashion stylists must work just as fast to change the models' hair and makeup to suit their outfits.

Often the makeup artist and the hairstylist are the same person; it is cheaper to hire one person with two skills than to hire two individuals. Fashion stylists usually work on a **freelance** basis and are hired for specific fashion shows or photo shoots. They must be prepared to travel to wherever there is work.

Main responsibilities of a fashion makeup artist and hairstylist

After makeup artists and hairstylists are hired for a fashion show or a photo shoot, they meet with the rest of the team for the project to discuss what is required. This group will include designers, photographers, and **lighting technicians**. The head fashion designer might instruct them to create a look to match an overall theme — for example, producing the illusion that models are from the Wild West or from the future. Stylists may also be asked to undertake special effects — for example, producing a windblown or suntanned look for a photo session.

Fashion model Claudia Schiffer (*seated*) talks over what is required for a fashion show with her makeup artist.

Good Points and Bad Points

"What I do like is the creative side of my work. A face is like a blank piece of paper, waiting for me to start work on it."

"I get tired of people telling me how glamorous my job must be, however, and how they would love to meet so many famous people. One face is very similar to another, and there is no time to chat when putting on someone's makeup."

One the other hand, the designer might prefer more natural-looking makeup and hairstyles in photographs for advertisements.

When a particular effect is required, the fashion stylist works out some ideas and discusses them with the rest of the team. Stylists may also practice their hair and makeup designs on models to achieve the best effect. When complex special effects are required, stylists work from sketches and photographs to make sure they create the right look to meet the needs of the head fashion designer.

A fashion designer (*center*) talks with a model (*left*) while a makeup artist covers the model's legs with base, a kind of tan powder.

On the day of a photo shoot or fashion runway show, stylists arrive early to set out their makeup and equipment. They make sure they have the correct hair products and curling irons and the right colors of eye shadow and blushes. Stylists check their notes about what work is to be done and discuss last-minute changes with the rest of the team. When the models arrive, stylists begin to transform their makeup and hair. Throughout photo shoots and fashion shows, they are on hand to repair makeup and hair and to adapt styles when necessary.

Main qualifications of a fashion makeup artist and hairstylist

Artistic skills

Stylists need to be able to visualize how their makeup and hairstyles will look before they begin work on the models. They use makeup in the same way that artists use paint — to create something beautiful.

Knowledge of tools of the trade

Stylists need to have good ideas, but they also should be able to turn these ideas into reality. They must be able to use different types of makeup in a professional way and style hair into whatever look is required. They have to keep up with changes in hairstyles and makeup and products for both. Because of safety issues, stylists need to know exactly how the products they use on models can affect the models' skin and hair.

At the Bridal Model contest in Tokyo, Japan, in 2004, makeup artists were on hand to carry out repair work. In this annual contest, more than sixty artists compete to coordinate make-up, hairstyling, **accessories**, and outfits.

Stamina

Fashion stylists spend most of the day on their feet, often working in uncomfortable conditions. They also have to carry around heavy cases full of makeup and equipment.

Tact and patience

To do their jobs well, stylists need to get along with everyone. Models may be nervous before a show, and stylists must help them relax so the stylist can apply their makeup and do their hair swiftly and well.

A supermodel during the 1970s, Lauren Hutton used the tricks she learned from forty years of working with the world's best makeup artists to create her own line of cosmetics and skin-care products.

fact file

Some fashion stylists attend cosmetology schools to learn about hairstyling or take courses in makeup. Others learn from working at makeup counters in stores and move up into fashion hairstyling and makeup. Others are taught by experienced stylists.

Reliability

Many stylists compete to work on fashion shows and photo shoots. Stylists must build a reputation for good work, punctuality, and never letting clients down.

Concentration

At a runway fashion show, people crowd the room where models prepare. Photographers snap pictures, fashion designers talk to journalists, and models and their stylists are everywhere. Stylists must focus on their work to get their models ready on time.

Vittorio Dalzetti

Vittorio has been working as a makeup artist for almost five years. He has always worked freelance, which means he is self-employed and has to find his own jobs. It was tough at first, but work has increased as he has become better known.

8:30 a.m. I'm enjoying my coffee and cleaning out my makeup box, throwing away any pieces of cotton balls or tissues that have found their way in there. I make a list of any products that will soon need replacing. I also check that everything is in the right place. Hunting for an eye shadow during a makeup session takes precious time and makes me appear disorganized.

10:15 a.m. Looking through some notes from a meeting yesterday, I think over ways of creating a 1940s look for a show. I dig out some of my fashion books and start jotting down ideas.

12:00 p.m. It has taken me a while, but I have some good ideas that I need to talk over at the next meeting with the show team. I hope they will fit in with the fashion designer's concept and the hair stylist's plans.

Fashion stylist Kevyn Aucoin worked on the makeup for movie stars, supermodels, and popular singers.

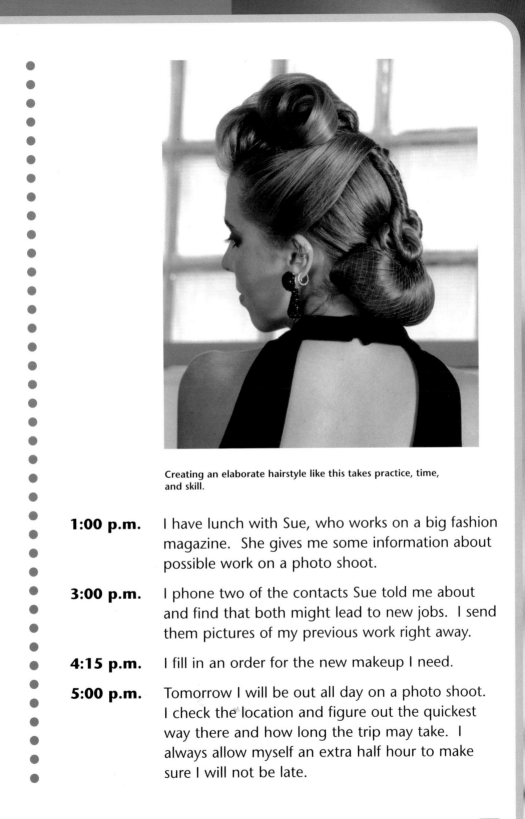

Creating an elaborate hairstyle like this takes practice, time, and skill.

1:00 p.m. I have lunch with Sue, who works on a big fashion magazine. She gives me some information about possible work on a photo shoot.

3:00 p.m. I phone two of the contacts Sue told me about and find that both might lead to new jobs. I send them pictures of my previous work right away.

4:15 p.m. I fill in an order for the new makeup I need.

5:00 p.m. Tomorrow I will be out all day on a photo shoot. I check the location and figure out the quickest way there and how long the trip may take. I always allow myself an extra half hour to make sure I will not be late.

Fashion Model

What is a fashion model?

Fashion models pose in clothing and **accessories**, displaying them as attractively as possible so that people will want to buy them. Clothing companies employ fashion models to wear garments and accessories, such as purses, shoes, gloves, and jewelry. The models work in a variety of situations, including performing in live fashion shows and posing for photographs for catalogs and magazines.

A model shows off a new design in a fashion show. Most models are young, tall and very slim.

Fashion modeling is usually a young person's job. Many female models begin their careers in their mid-teens, sometimes as young as fourteen. Male models start a little older. Both women and men tend to be tall and slim with appealing features.

Some models do not fit this standard. Known as character models, they include older people and people who may be disabled or shorter or heavier than most models. They usually

Cybill Shepherd: From Model to Actress

Born in 1950, Cybill Shepherd began modeling in her late teens. After winning Tennessee's Model of the Year contest, at eighteen, she rapidly became a top model, posing on the cover of many fashion magazines. Her appearance on the cover of *Glamour*, in 1969, caught a movie director's attention. He cast Shepherd in a major role in *The Last Picture Show,* a movie that became a classic. She has continued to model and to act in movies, on television, and on stage.

Some models are chosen for the look of specific body parts. This model's beautiful hands gained her a place in an ad.

have strong or interesting faces that draw the viewer's attention. Character models often pose for catalogs and advertisements in magazines.

Modeling has a glamorous image. Becoming a full-time professional model is difficult, however. Many young women and men compete for very few jobs. Most models work part-time and have other jobs to bring in steady income.

Main responsibilities of a fashion model

Most models find work through modeling agencies. These agencies choose models they think will appeal to their clients and can fulfill those clients' advertising needs. The agency shows photographs and descriptions of their models to clients. The client may then choose an agency's model, who must be prepared to take all sorts of different work. The model may be needed to:

A stylist works on this model's hair. Professional models need to make sure they look their best all the time, which can be expensive.

- model in a fashion show. Major fashion shows take place in big cities such as London, New York, Paris, and Milan in Italy. Before a show, models have to rehearse **runway** routines. These performances can be complicated, with models dancing to music and

Good Points and Bad Points

"I enjoy modeling. I'm not rich or famous, but I do some modeling for fashion shows and meet some interesting people. A couple of photographers also use me regularly to pose for pictures in catalogs."

"Keeping myself looking good costs a fortune. My hair has to be cut and dyed much more often than if I worked in an office. I also spend a lot of money on skin-care products and makeup. I don't do this because I'm vain, but because I have to look my best if I'm going to get work."

displaying clothes in a group. Models must quickly switch outfits during a show and need to practice these rapid changes of clothes, hairstyles, and make-up beforehand. During a show, they follow these routines to display the clothes to the audience.

- model for fashion photographs. Models may pose in a photography studio or in unusual places like factories, car showrooms, or airports. They may also model outside in warm, sunny climates or in the snow and ice. Photography sessions can last for hours while the photographer adjusts clothes, lighting, and the model's position. Models may pose for ads in fashion and other magazines; model clothing, accessories, and shoes for **mail-order catalogs**; and pose for posters and advertisements.

Fashion houses employ show-room models and pay them a regular salary. Models in show-rooms try on clothes so that designers can alter the outfit according to their vision of the garment. Models also wear clothes to show to buyers, customers, and fashion journalists. In addition, they talk about the details of the clothes and answer questions. Showroom models also work at large fashion shows, although many fashion houses use agency models for this type of work.

Customers can see how clothes look on fashion models in mail-order catalogs and easily imagine how the clothes might look on them.

Main qualifications of a fashion model

Attractive physical appearance

Models need to be of a certain height, weight, and age, with the type of looks that are currently popular. One year, fair-skinned models may be in demand; the next year, models of mixed ethnic backgrounds may be popular. Weight changes can mean losing work, so they need to make sure they do not gain even a few pounds.

Determination

Good looks and the right build are not enough for a successful modeling career. Only people who are prepared to put their careers before everything else in life are likely to succeed. The careers of even the most successful models rarely last longer than a few years.

Commitment

Models must be prepared to work long hours and travel long distances, often on short notice. They spend a lot of time following other people's instructions, standing or walking in a certain way.

Stamina

The work is tough and very tiring; at times, it may also be uncomfortably hot or cold. Models always have to smile, however, and look as if they are having a great time.

Originally seen as a woman's job, modeling has now become a male occupation, too. The same rules and pressures apply, however — models must be tall, slim, and good-looking.

Here, models relax at a knitting party organized by an agency in New York. A sense of humor is important in the tough world of fashion modeling.

fact file

A successful career in modeling depends on hard work, natural talent, and a great deal of luck. Models should understand the basics of clothing, makeup, and style. They must also work constantly to keep their skin flawless and their hair clean, healthy, and attractive.

Financial skills

Most models are self-employed, and their careers are often short. They need to **budget** their earnings well.

Confidence

Models need to believe in their own talent and ability to cope positively with disappointments.

Good humor and the ability to get along with others

Even top models cannot behave badly and throw tantrums. Word spreads quickly in the fashion world when a model is difficult to work with. A bad reputation soon leads to a shortage of work.

A day in the life of a fashion model

Lauren Moss

Lauren is eighteen years old and has been working as a fashion model for more than a year. She sent some photographs of herself to an agency that now finds work for her. She also has a part-time job in the evenings at a restaurant, which she hopes to give up in a few months when her modeling work has increased.

6:30 a.m. The alarm goes off, and I get up and jump into the shower. I live at home, and my parents don't charge me any rent. They really support me — I don't think I could manage without them.

7:30 a.m. I finish doing my hair and makeup, and I pack my overnight bag. I have a cup of coffee and a bowl of cereal. Today, I'm off to work in a **trade exhibition** of outdoor fashions. The event lasts for three days, with four fashion shows every day. We will be modeling hiking boots, jackets, and warm sweaters and pants.

8:00 a.m. I meet a couple of other models at the train station.

10:30 a.m. We arrive at the exhibition center and are shown the runway and changing rooms. We try on our clothes, which is just as well because a couple of my sweaters have to be changed.

Models have to keep themselves slim and fit if they want to continue finding work.

A successful fashion show needs to be thoroughly rehearsed. Changes have to be quick, and any damage to makeup and hair must be repaired in a few seconds. Despite their hurry, models have to look prepared and professional.

11:30 a.m. Rehearsals begin. I have a dozen or so outfit changes, and I have to make sure I can do them quickly. The moves on the runway are very complicated, more like dancing than walking.

1:00 p.m. Sandwiches are brought in, and we collapse for ten minutes before continuing with the rehearsal. There are eight of us, and we all seem to work well together.

3:00 p.m. Our changing rooms are very chilly, probably because the heat will not be turned on until the show opens tomorrow.

5:30 p.m. The place is now freezing but we're still at work, trying on clothes and practicing our moves. The show is gradually coming together.

7:30 p.m. The bus has arrived to take us to the hotel, where I'm going to take a very hot bath.

Fashion Photographer

Fashion photographers take pictures of fashion models. They may work at huge fashion shows, taking pictures of the models as they walk down a **runway** wearing the latest designs, or they may work in studios, creating images for advertisements and catalogs. They may even work both places in the same day or week. Whatever the location, a fashion photographer's job is to make both the models and the fashions look attractive.

Only a small part of a fashion photographer's job, however, is actually taking pictures. Photographers work with models, makeup and hair stylists, and **lighting engineers** to prepare for **photo shoots**. Making sure that the clothes, models, lighting, and background all look exactly right before starting to take pictures. All this arranging takes a lot of time.

Fashion photographers also spend a lot of time trying to contact possible employers and find work. Most fashion photographers are **freelancers**, which means they are self-employed. They work for a number of different clients and receive a fee for each job.

This fashion photographer works in a well-lit studio, producing clothing ads for a local department store. Her photos appear in the store's newspaper advertisements.

Richard Avedon

Richard Avedon was famous throughout the world not only for his fashion photography but for his pictures of celebrities and everyday people. Born in 1923, he began taking photos for fashion magazines *Harper's Bazaar* in 1946 and *Vogue* in 1966. His later portraits of celebrities revealed much of their personalities. Avedon's photographs have been shown in major museums and art galleries. He died in 2004.

A photographer measures the light levels around a fashion model during a shoot. The right lighting is vital to the quality of a photographer's work.

Sometimes, a client will give a fashion photographer a contract for a long-term job.

Like other photographers, fashion photographers may use different types of cameras. Many use traditional cameras that record images on film. They either develop the film themselves or take it to a film laboratory. Others rely on digital cameras that record images electronically. Photographers download the images onto a computer.

There are two types of fashion photography:

- Runway photography involves taking pictures at fashion shows. Photographers cover the **haute couture** and **ready-to-wear** fashion shows. They may photograph several shows on the same day, working from early morning until late at night. Photographers arrive at a **venue** early to get a good position. Between shows, they move their equipment to the next venue. They may be hired by a newspaper or other client, or they may try to sell their pictures to a publication later.

- In advertising and editorial photography, fashion photographers take pictures of models and their clothes. They snap these photos in a photographic studio or in other locations. Stores, publications, and **mail-order catalogs** all hire fashion photographers.

A studio photo shoot gets started. Fashion models, assistants, and equipment are all expensive. Photographers must work fast if they want to keep project costs down.

Good Points and Bad Points

"One week, I have so much work I barely get any sleep, and the next week, the phone never seems to ring. I love the challenge of coming up with new ideas and working with models."

"Fashion photography is not a job for the nervous, however. You never know when your next job will be."

On some jobs, fashion photographers need assistants to run errands, pack and unpack equipment, and help set up **props** and **backdrops**. Photographers hire assistants on a day-to-day basis. Most young photographers begin their careers as assistants.

Fashion photographers own their basic equipment, including cameras and lights. They may also rent equipment, such as special cameras, lights, and **lenses**, for specific jobs. Cameras and other supplies are very expensive. Photographers typically own thousands of dollars' worth of equipment. As they become better known — and better paid — they sell off old cameras and buy newer ones.

Well-established fashion photographers have their own studios for their work. There, they can keep all their equipment. Most other photographers rent studios by the day and haul their equipment there.

Photographers chat with models backstage at a fashion show. Photographers must talk with many people to find work.

Main qualifications of a fashion photographer

Artistic skills

Fashion photographers need to be creative even when working under intense pressure and in crowded conditions. They must know what lines, colors, and forms will make a good photograph.

Technical skills

Technology for photography changes all the time, and fashion photographers need to keep up with the newest equipment. They must know which lens, which light, and even which camera will create the effect that they want and that their clients will like.

Today, fashion photography can involve visits to exotic places. While conditions in the studio can be controlled, photo shoots away from the studio bring additional problems of weather and lighting.

Strong interest in fashion

No one wants to use a photographer who is unaware of fashion trends and does not have good ideas about how to show styles at their best.

Computer skills

Today, most professional photographers use digital cameras. They can improve pictures on a computer and make changes such as removing unwanted shadows.

Before taking the final photos, the photographer checks out a picture of his early work on the shoot. He must make sure he has made the right changes to the lighting.

fact file

There is no one way to become a fashion photographer. Some people attend a technical or an art school or go to many photography **seminars**. The most common way is to assist fashion photographers in their work. The assistants may not be paid; the skills and knowledge they acquire from the job is often more than enough pay. Starting photographers must build a **portfolio** of their best pictures to show possible clients.

Business skills

Most fashion photographers manage their work alone. They must make their own appointments and meet their clients' deadlines. They must decide upon the amount of money to charge for a job, making sure their work pays enough for their business costs and for their living expenses. These tasks take time and organizational skills.

Interpersonal skills

Fashion photographers work with a wide variety of people, from models to lighting engineers to magazine editors. They must communicate what they want to their models, stylists, and assistants and respond to their clients' ideas and needs.

Will Duncan

Will is a freelance fashion photographer. His interest in photography began when he was a teenager. After taking a photography course in college, he was offered a job as an assistant to a fashion photographer. A short time ago, he set up his own freelance business.

8:00 a.m.   I'm in my van with a map and my assistant Roy, who is driving. He has been doing a lot of work for me recently, so he's getting to know how I operate. We are off to a chocolate factory for a magazine fashion shoot. In the fashion world, everybody is trying to think of something different, and this setting is what the magazine editor wants.

9:00 a.m.   Roy unloads the equipment. I go find the fashion editor and the factory manager.

9:45 a.m.   We are all coming up with some ideas about how to pose the models. We want to make sure no one is hurt by the factory equipment during the shoot. The factory manager assures us that none of the machinery will be working during the shoot.

10:30 a.m.   We're using some volunteer factory workers in protective smocks in the shots. The models will pose in their different outfits with the workers in the background.

11:00 a.m.   Shooting starts. I'm very glad Roy is here. He is quick to move the lighting and equipment wherever I tell him. He has also come up with some good ideas for interesting shots.

2:30 p.m. I use my laptop computer to show the editor the shots I have taken on my digital camera so she can decide what else she needs. The production staff are definitely less excited than they were. They are tired; most of them seem to wish they had stuck to making chocolate.

4:00 p.m. I'm back at the laptop computer. Luckily, the editor likes my shots, and the day ends on a positive note.

5:00 p.m. Roy and I load the van for the trip home.

A photographer takes pictures of a fashion model on a beach. Assistants hold up reflectors to shine light onto the model's face.

Photographers crowd around the runway to get a photo of fashion model Kate Moss. After the show, the photographers must get their pictures to their clients as quickly as possible.

Fashion Writer

What is a fashion writer?

Fashion writers produce articles on fashion for magazines, newspapers, and web sites. They are an important link between fashion designers, clothing and **accessory** manufacturers, and members of the public. Through their writing, they inform people about **trends** in clothing styles and where to buy these clothes.

Fashion is big business. At one time, clothes were usually homemade. People threw them away only when the clothes became so worn that they could not be mended. Today, many people do not wait for clothes to fall apart to buy new ones. They buy new outfits as soon as a new style of clothing appears in stores.

Clothes in the latest colors and styles fill today's stores. Many people find out the "must haves" for the next few months through newspapers, magazines, television programs, and sometimes the Internet. These **media** display the latest clothing trends and show celebrities wearing the new styles. Fashion manufacturers use the yearly change of seasons as a reason to develop new styles of clothing. People who want up-to-date styles buy clothing year-round.

Fashion magazines bring the latest trends to their readers.

Keeping in *Vogue*

Wealthy people who can afford **haute couture** enjoy keeping up with the latest styles — and so do many of the less wealthy. There are fashion magazines for many income levels. The most influential fashion magazine in the world, however, is *Vogue*, begun in 1892 in Paris. By the 1920s, *Vogue* was having a strong influence on the fashion scene, promoting French fashions to readers. Today, the magazine is published in many different languages and read throughout the world. Many fashion writers would like to work for *Vogue*, but only a few ever reach that lofty goal.

The cover of *Vogue* from 1929. Styles may have changed over the years, but the job of the fashion magazine has always been to cover the latest trends.

Many fashion writers work on a **freelance** basis, hired to write about specific events or styles. Others work full- or part-time for businesses. Fashion writers can provide articles for several kinds of publications or for a growing number of fashion web sites. There are monthly magazines devoted entirely to the latest fashions, too. Teen and women's magazines boast large fashion sections, while national newspapers run weekly fashion features. Some television shows focus on fashions and need writers, too.

Main responsibilities of a fashion writer

Fashion writers need to know exactly what is going on in the fashion world. They get this information in the following ways:

Fashion writers attend shows to view the newest styles and meet professionally with other journalists, designers, and buyers.

- by making close contacts in the industry — getting to know people who work in different areas of fashion and keeping in regular touch
- by attending fashion shows and **trade exhibitions** and interviewing people working in the industry
- by reviewing information from the **public relations** (PR) departments of **fashion houses** and large stores
- by meeting with designers from fashion houses
- by carrying out their own research by reading about fashion

Good Points and Bad Points

"Being a fashion writer means I get to review exciting fashion shows and interview creative people in the industry."

"My work is a lot of fun, but I still have to make sure all my deadlines are met, and these time limits add to the pressure of the job. I often work evenings, which sometimes gets very tiring."

Using the information they have gathered, fashion writers discuss future articles with their **editors**. The writers and editors want to make sure they cover what people will want to read. Editors make the final decisions about what is published and may make last-minute changes to a publication.

The editor decides on the length of an article before the writer begins, and the writer must keep to that word limit. The writer also must finish the work by a certain deadline, which is a set date, so the magazine or newspaper can be printed on time.

Writers also work closely with photographers to ensure that the photos accompanying an article are just right. To achieve this, the writers must:

- agree with the photographers on which models and locations to use
- contact fashion houses or stores to supply clothes for the models
- select the photographs to accompany the article

Top fashion writers travel around the world to fashion shows. They fly to New York; London; Paris; and Milan, Italy, to cover the important fashion shows.

Main qualifications of a fashion writer

Excellent fashion sense

Every season, clothing manufacturers and fashion houses produce outfits in new styles and colors. Fashion-magazine readers want to know well in advance what is going to be in the stores in the coming months, and they rely on fashion writers to tell them this. Fashion houses, manufacturers, and stores all want **publicity** and work hard to persuade writers to write about them and their creations. Fashion writers need to see beyond the glamour of the fashion world to judge what styles are likely to appeal to their readers and sell well.

Writing skills

Fashion writers need to pack a lot of information into their articles. They also must write in a way that readers find interesting and easy to follow.

Networking

Fashion writers must make excellent contacts within the fashion industry to make sure they hear all the latest news as quickly as possible. Their clients and readers count on knowing the most up-to-date information.

Fashion writers must work with the rest of the creative team when selecting pictures. Because they actually attended the fashion show, the writers know which photos best reflect the designs shown.

Organizational skills

Fashion writers must plan their time carefully to cope with busy schedules and meet deadlines for articles.

The influential editor of American *Vogue*, Anna Wintour (*left*) talks to top fashion designer Donna Karan. Contacts are crucial in the fashion field.

Energy and enthusiasm

Life is busy for fashion writers both in and out of the office. Fashion writing is definitely not a job that starts at nine in the morning and ends at five in the evening. It often involves staying late at the office to finish work on time. Writers also often spend several evenings each week meeting contacts for meals and attending fashion events.

Computer skills

Today, all journalists work on computers. They write articles on laptops while working away from the office and E-mail them to editors.

fact file

Employers usually only consider someone with a college degree for a position as a fashion writer. They often prefer people with college majors in journalism or fashion merchandising; having both is a real plus. Many writers start as **interns** for the fashion sections of newspapers or for fashion magazines. They may also start as freelance writers.

A day in the life of a fashion writer

Amy Moran

Amy is a fashion writer with a national newspaper. Her first job after college was as an intern on a local newspaper. The team working on the paper was small, and because of Amy's interest in fashion, she was soon given the fashion page to write. Her next job was as assistant fashion editor on a regional paper, and from there she went on to her present job.

8:00 a.m. I'm in the office early to work on an article that I need to give to my editor by noon.

9:00 a.m. My phone begins to ring. I tell the receptionist I'm not taking calls. It may sound harsh, but unless I'm firm, I could be on the phone all day long and get no work done.

9:30 a.m. I check my calendar to make sure I have not forgotten to do anything important.

10:00 a.m. A photographer arrives with photos taken for my article. We choose three or four possible images together.

11:45 a.m. I eat lunch at my desk as I check through the article and then phone my editor. He wants to see me to talk over how the article should look and discuss my ideas for the next month or so.

12:30 p.m. I hop into my car. At the end of each semester, a local university holds a fashion show that displays its students' best designs. I find that watching these are a great way of discovering new designers.

4:00 p.m. The show was fun, and I pick out three students whose designs I would like to write about.

4:15 p.m.   I interview the students while the photographer takes some shots of their designs.

5:30 p.m.   I decide to go home and spend the evening working on my article about the students.

9:00 p.m.   At last, I have hot bath, a pizza, and a chance to relax in front of the television before bed and another early start tomorrow.

Writers and guests attend a fashion show given by the students of designer Vivienne Westwood. Here, a model shows off one of Westwood's creations.

Writers and photographers scramble for good positions to hear and photograph fashion designers and their models.

Retail Buyer

What is a retail buyer?

Retail **buyers** select and order all the clothing and other goods that a store sells. They must know before a clothing style appears on the sales floor exactly what will sell. The range of goods available in stores today is huge. Retail buyers choose the style of every item.

Departments stores want to sell their products quickly so they can make money. But sales depend on buyers. Here, holiday shoppers hurry through the aisles of Macy's in New York City during after-Thanksgiving sales.

Major chain stores have branches in most cities, and they may appear to sell the same clothes in each one. The style of items for sale may be different from location to location, however. Styles that sell out quickly in a lively city or wealthy suburb may stay on the shelves a long time in a quiet small town or a poorer area. Retail buyers have a huge amount of responsibility for the success of a store or chain of stores. Neither eye-catching displays nor a dedicated sales staff can sell unwanted goods. If a store does not provide customers with what they want, they will shop somewhere else. Retail buyers need to know exactly what customers like and what styles they want to buy.

The Retail Revolution

In 1838, Aristide Boucicaut opened the first department store, called Bon Marché, in Paris, France. It displayed goods in different departments, all for sale at a set price. The store promised customers their money back or an item in exchange if they were not satisfied. Until then, most stores would not exchange goods or promise that they were well made. In 1846, Alexander Turney Stewart built his "Marble Palace" in New York City. It was the first department store in the United States, selling women's clothes brought from Europe and holding fashion shows for customers.

Retail buyers must check for the quality of their purchases. Their stores' customers will be sure to do so. If shoppers are not satisfied, they will stop buying at that particular store.

Retail buyers need to keep up-to-date with the latest styles and developments of fashion. They must also keep current with population changes in their area. If a new apartment building is opening or new factories or offices are built, new people may move into an area. These new residents may bring different needs and style requirements that stores should respond to.

Fashion buyers must keep up with the latest fasion trends. To do so, they:

- read fashion magazines, articles, and web sites
- attend fashion shows and **trade exhibitions**
- meet staff from **fashion houses** and manufacturers
- closely watch what is selling at other stores across the country and what **haute couture** and **ready-to-wear** fashion styles could be adapted for their stores

Fashion buyers also work for fabric stores. Choosing the right fabric at a reasonable price is part of their job. They also look for fashionable prints and colors.

Stores must order products long before the goods appear in stores. Retail buyers' work must begin even earlier. First, they must find out the store's **budget** for the purchase of the season's goods.

Good Points and Bad Points

"I travel quite a lot with my job, which I enjoy, because it means every day is different. I like identifying new **trends** and making decisions about what to buy."

"I do worry about the responsibilities I have — including spending a lot of money that isn't mine. I need to be adventurous and find clothes that are new and different, but I also have to put myself in my customers' place and think of what they want. If I make too many bad choices, I could be out of a job."

Some buyers fly around the world looking for the right products.

Along with the fashion sales manager and other store managers, they also figure out what types of clothing will probably sell well.

Second, buyers attend fashion shows to look for the latest styles. They also meet with manufacturers to find the styles that are right for their particular store or chain of stores. They discuss the prices for each amount of clothing they wish to buy from a manufacturer. Costs usually depend on the size of an order — the larger the order, the lower the price of an individual item.

Third, buyers make suggestions to the store about what to buy. Once the store decides to follow those suggestions, the retail buyers place an order with the manufacturer. When the order arrives, buyers make sure that:

- all products have been delivered to the right place at the right time
- the right number of styles have been made in the correct colors and sizes
- the clothing and accessories are all well made

Main qualifications of a retail buyer

Up-to-date knowledge of fashion
Buyers must combine a good sense of fashion with a sure knowledge of the type of clothes their customers will like. They cannot purchase clothes in extremely modern styles if they know their customers will always choose more traditional fashions.

Strong local market awareness
A knowledge of what customers will buy comes from looking carefully at how well items have sold in the store in the past and talking to local sales managers. With computers linked to cash registers, it is easy to track sales of specific items. Retail buyers must also be aware of the local **economy**. Will their customers have enough income to buy higher-priced goods, or will they need to wait for the sales to buy?

Sales meetings give buyers a chance to get up-to-date with sales managers and other staff members.

Communication skills
Buyers spend a lot of time dealing with people and working on agreements. They must have a friendly manner and be able to explain clearly exactly what they are looking for to both assistant buyers and manufacturers.

Commitment
Buyers must be prepared to work long hours, travel a great deal, sometimes in other countries, and spend time away from home.

Items that do not sell quickly have to be sold at a reduced price. Buyers try to make sure most items sell at full price.

Organizational skills

A buyer's days are busy and involve meetings with different people in different places. Buyers need to plan their time carefully and keep to a strict schedule.

Decision-making skills

Retail buyers must be willing to decide quickly whether certain items will sell in the future. To make sure their store stays up-to-date, buyers may have to take risks on unknown styles and hope that those fashions sell.

fact file

Colleges and technical schools offer degrees in marketing and retail management that can lead eventually to a job as a buyer. Graduates still need to spend time selling items in the store, supervising staff, and tracking **stock** before they are allowed to become assistant buyers and eventually senior retail buyers.

Julia James

Julia is senior fashion buyer with a large department store. She joined the company as a sales assistant and worked her way up to the position of buyer.

9:00 a.m. There's a lot to do because this afternoon I'm leaving on a trip to visit fashion houses and manufacturers in different parts of Europe.

We sell a wide range of fashions, from teenage styles to exclusive evening and wedding dresses. I'm in charge of overall fashion buying, and I have a team of three buyers working with me. One of them will be coming on the trip.

9:30 a.m. I attend a meeting with other fashion buyers and managers. There's a lot to discuss, including the upcoming sale. Each department manager reports on his or her plans. Sales are a good way to bring in customers and get rid of old stock. We can't afford to lose too much money, though, so we must set our prices carefully.

11:30 a.m. Last-minute changes to my schedule mean that an important meeting with a manufacturer has to be changed. He is one of the key people I want to see, so I'm on the phone for the next couple of hours rescheduling three days of my trip.

1:30 p.m. I take a late lunch as I check through my paperwork and memorize as many facts and figures as I can. My budget is tight, and I must spend my money wisely.

2:30 p.m. The manager of the wedding-dress department calls to find out if we can make sure a certain style of dress will arrive in three months. The dresses are made individually for each customer; three months is a very tight deadline. I make some phone calls and check delivery dates.

3:45 p.m. We're on our way to the airport. I make some notes in the taxi and discuss some ideas for the next few days with my coworker.

5:15 p.m. The flight will be called in the next five minutes, so it's time to find our passports and boarding passes.

Designer Victor Alfaro (*left*) works to convince fashion buyer June Horne (*center*) that his dresses will sell well.

A successful sale is always good news for a retail buyer.

Glossary

accessories – items or objects of dress or fashion, such as shoes, handbags, gloves, and jewelry, which, while often unnecessary, enhance outfits or main articles of clothing

backdrops – backgrounds of scenery or designs, usually painted on cloth and hung behind furnishings and props that have been set up for photo shoots or theater productions

boutique – a small shop specializing in certain types of fashion or beauty products or services

budget – (n) a specific amount of money made available for a particular use or purpose (v) to assign necessary or reasonable amounts of available money to meet particular expenses

buyer – a person employed to select and purchase the merchandise that will be sold at a store or through some other method of marketing

chrome – a silver-colored metal with a mirrorlike surface

customer service – a company department or group of employees responsible for the efficient and cost-effective delivery of goods and services as well as for customers' satisfaction with goods and services

design program – computer software that allows a designer to visualize and manipulate ideas on-screen before starting the actual production process

economy – the conditions of an area related to the availability, use, and management of wealth, such as money, natural resources, and human resources

editors – people whose job is to select, refine, and assemble written material for publication

enhance – to improve the quality, beauty, or effectiveness of something

fashion houses – establishments that each represent the work of a prominent fashion designer or a group of collaborating designers

freelance – self-employed and free to work for more than one client

haute couture – high fashion, the most expensive level of the fashion industry, involving the creation of individual, often trend-setting, designs

henna – a reddish-brown dye that comes from the leaves of a plant found in Asia and North Africa

interns – workers who are employed as trainees to learn a skill or a trade on the job under the guidance of an experienced professional

kohl – a cosmetic powder used, especially in the Middle East, to darken the eyelids

lenses – the curved pieces of glass in cameras, used to focus images and control the amount of light that hits the film when shooting a photograph

lighting engineers (technicians) – skilled professionals who determine the type and placement of lighting equipment for photo shoots

mail-order catalogs – publications containing pictures and descriptions of products for sale, from which customers can place orders for direct delivery, instead of shopping at stores

mannequin – a life-size, manufactured model of a human body, used mainly to display clothing

market – a segment of a population involved in the buying and selling of particular goods and services

mass production – the process of manufacturing products in large quantities, usually using machines

media – channels of communication, such as newspapers or television, that distribute information to the public

paisley – a pattern of small, curved shapes with intricate artistic details

photo shoots – scheduled sessions during which series of photographs are taken for particular uses

portfolio – a collection of original work that demonstrates the skills of an artist, photographer, or writer

props – short for "properties," which are items or objects added to create attractive or realistic arrangements for displays or photographs

public relations – actions performed and statements made by businesses to encourage favorable public opinion

publicity – information spread, usually through the media, to make the public more aware of certain people or events

ready-to-wear – a name for designer clothing that is produced in small quantities and sold in expensive stores

runway – a narrow platform on which models walk to display clothing during a fashion show

seminars – study groups or scheduled meetings to discuss information on particular topics

separates – pieces of clothing, such as skirts, slacks, sweaters, and blouses, worn interchangeably to create many different outfits or combinations

stock – a supply of goods available for purchase; inventory

three-dimensional – having length, width, and height, or depth

trade exhibitions (trade fairs) – a large display of objects to the general public or to special audiences by businesses that produce similar goods or have certain interests in common

trends – current style preferences

venue – the place where an event or gathering, such as a fashion show, is being or will be held

Further Information

This book does not cover all of the jobs in the fashion industry. Many jobs are not mentioned, including clothing pattern maker, fashion sales representative, and costume designer. This book does, however, give you an idea of what working in the fashion industry is like.

The fashion world is exciting and fast-paced and can be very glamorous. It's important to remember, however, that there are many more people wanting to work in the fashion industry than there are jobs available. It takes talent, hard work, determination, and a great deal of luck to succeed as a model, fashion designer, makeup artist, photographer, or almost any other fashion profession.

The only way to decide if working in the fashion industry is right for you is to find out what the work involves. Read as much as you can about fashion careers and talk to people, especially people you know, who work in this industry.

When you are in middle school or high school, a teacher or career counselor might be able to help you arrange some work experience in a certain career. For the fashion industry, that experience could mean helping out at a clothing store, visiting a design school, or watching a fashion photo shoot to see how people working in these professions spend their time.

Books

Careers without College: Makeup Artist
Kathryn A. Quinlan
(Capstone, 1999)

Choosing a Career as a Model
Cheryl Tobey
(Rosen, 2001)

Discovering Careers for Your Future: Fashion
Robert Green
(Ferguson, 2004)

I Want to Be a Fashion Designer
Stephanie Maze
(Harcourt, 2000)

Web Sites

The ABCs of Fashion Merchandising
www.fashionschool
 review.com/fashion-
 merchandising-basics.
 html

Fashion Careers
www.fashion-schools.org/
 fashion-careers.htm

How to become a fashion photographer
www.fashion.net/howto/
 photography

Useful Addresses

Display Designer

National Association of Display
  Industries, Inc.
3595 Sheridan Street, Suite 200
Hollywood, FL 33021
Tel: (954) 893-7225
www.nadi-global.com

National Association of Visual
  Merchandisers
15304 Rainbow One, Suite 201
Austin, TX 78734
Tel: (512) 266-0224
www.visualmerch.com

Fashion and Related Industries

Fashion Group International, Inc.
8 West 40th Street, 7th floor
New York, NY 10018
Tel: (212) 302-5511
www.fgi.org

Fashion Designer

Council of Fashion Designers of America
1412 Broadway, Suite 2006
New York, NY 10018
Tel: (212) 302-1821
www.cfda.com

International Association of Clothing
  Designers & Executives
124 West 93rd Street, Suite 3E
New York, NY 10025
Tel: (212) 222-2082
www.iacde.com

Fashion Makeup Artist and Hairstylist

National Cosmetology Association
401 N. Michigan Avenue, 22nd floor
Chicago, IL 60611
Tel: (312) 527-6765
www.ncacares.org

Fashion Photographer

American Society of Media
  Photographers, Inc.
150 North 2nd Street
Philadelphia, PA 19106
Tel: (215) 451-2767
www.asmp.org

Fashion Writer

American Society of Journalists
  and Authors
1501 Broadway, Suite 302
New York, NY 10036
Tel: (212) 997-0947
www.asja.org

Retail Buyer

National Retail Federation
325 7th Street NW, Suite 1100
Washington, DC 20004
Tel: (202) 783-7971 (800) 673-4692
www.nrf.com

Index